Classic Collection

TREASURE ISLAND

ROBERT LOUIS STEVENSON

Adapted by Ronne Randall • Illustrated by Robert Dunn

QEB Publishing

The Old Sea Dog Arrives at the Inn

My name is Jim Hawkins, and I've been asked to tell the story of Treasure Island—so I will. It happened years ago, when I was just a boy helping my parents run the Admiral Benbow Inn. My father was sick, so it was my job to help my mother.

I remember as if it were yesterday, the day the weathered old sailor came looking for lodgings. His hands and face were scarred and filthy, and he wore a soiled blue coat. A greasy black ponytail hung across his shoulder. He dragged an old sea chest behind him—and never opened it all the time he was with us. And I remember how, on that first day, he sang an old sea song:

"Fifteen men on the dead man's chest,
Yo-ho-ho and a bottle of rum!"

The sailor's name was Billy Bones. He drank a great deal of rum, often disturbing other guests with his loud, drunken singing and grisly tales. But if any other seafaring man came into the inn, Bones looked worried. Indeed, he promised to pay me fourpence a month to keep a lookout for a one-legged sailor whom he spoke of with dread. Although Bones gave me my fourpenny piece when I asked, he didn't pay for his lodgings after the first week. My poor mother never dared ask him for what he owed. Only Dr. Livesey, who came to look after my father, stood up to Billy Bones.

One frosty morning, a man came to the inn looking for his "mate, Bill." When Billy Bones saw the stranger, he turned pale.

"Black Dog!" he gasped.

The two sat down together and sent me to fetch rum for them. I brought it, then stood outside the door, trying to hear what they were saying. All I could hear was a low rumble, until Billy shouted, "No! No, no, no, no, and that's the end of it!"

There was a crash of tables and chairs falling over, followed by the clash of steel. Black Dog ran out, blood pouring from his shoulder, followed by Billy Bones. Both men had their cutlasses drawn.

When Billy came back, he was unsteady on his feet.

"I must get away from here!" he cried. Then he collapsed. Mother and I sent for Dr. Livesey, who said Billy had suffered a stroke.

"He must rest," said the doctor, "and should have no strong drink. It could bring on another stroke, which would kill him." All three of us battled to get him to bed.

Billy was soon awake and clamoring for rum. I told him what the doctor had said, but he didn't care. When I brought him the rum, he said, "I can tell you this, Jim, because you're the only one I can trust."

He told me he had been first mate for a pirate called Captain Flint, who had given him a treasure map before he died. Billy kept the map in his old sea chest. Now his old shipmates were after it.

The Black Spot

My father died the next night, so I forgot about Billy Bones's troubles, though Mother and I made sure we gave him regular doses of the medicine Dr. Livesey had left for him. Despite the medicine, he seemed to get weaker each day, and he still drank vast amounts of rum.

The day after my father's funeral, a blind man with a cane and a green shade over his eyes hobbled up to the inn. He asked to be taken to Billy Bones, who was sitting in the parlor in a drunken stupor.

"Here's a friend for you, Billy," I said, leading the blind man toward him.

Billy raised his head, and with one look his drunkenness vanished, leaving him sober but too weak even to stand. "Blind Pew!" he whispered.

"Boy," said Blind Pew to me, "take his left hand by the wrist and bring it near to my right."

I did as he asked, and saw him pass something from his hand to Billy's.

"Now that's done," he said, then turned and left. I could hear the tap-tap-tap of his cane as he walked quickly down the street. As soon as he was gone, Billy looked at the paper Blind Pew had given him.

"The black spot!" he cried in fear. "It's a warning, Jim. It means my old shipmates are coming to get me. They'll be here by ten o'clock." Once again he tried to stand, but his body reeled and he toppled over, falling flat on the floor. I knew at once that he was dead.

I lost no time in telling my mother what I knew about Billy Bones and his sea chest. If his shipmates came back, we could be in danger. Still, we decided to open the chest in case there was any money in it, for Bones had owed us a great deal for his bed and board.

The chest was full of tobacco, trinkets, some papers wrapped in oilskin, and a canvas bag filled with coins. We were counting the money when we heard the tap-tap-tap of a cane outside the window, and footsteps close behind. Blind Pew had returned—with more pirates!

Mother grabbed the sack of coins, I took the papers, and we fled. We managed to find a hiding place close by, from where we could see the pirates breaking into the inn. Within minutes, someone stuck his head out of an upstairs window.

"They've emptied the chest," he cried. "The papers have gone. Find the boy!"

Just then we heard the sound of hooves, and a shot rang out. Five soldiers on horseback came galloping toward the inn, and the pirates fled—all except Blind Pew. Bewildered, he stumbled right into the soldiers' path and was trampled by their horses.

The soldiers were anxious to see if Mother and I were all right.

"What were they after?" asked an officer.

"I think it was this," I replied, showing him the packet of papers. "We'd better take it to Dr. Livesey for safekeeping."

The Captain's Papers

Worried for my safety, one of the soldiers escorted me to Dr. Livesey's house. The doctor was having dinner with his friend Squire Trelawney when I arrived. Both of them were very interested in my story, and together we eagerly opened the oilskin packet.

Inside they found a notebook, which had lists of dates, ships' names, places, and sums of money.

"It's the rogue's account book!" cried Squire Trelawney, rifling through the pages. "These are all the ships they raided, the amounts they stole, and where they buried the treasure. There must be a map as well!"

And indeed there was. It had been sealed in several places, so Dr. Livesey opened it carefully. A thrill went through me as I looked at the treasure map Bones had spoken of. The doctor and the squire were excited, too.

"Livesey," said Squire Trelawney, "I am leaving for Bristol tomorrow, and I want you to come with me. In less than a month we can outfit a ship and assemble a crew. You, Jim, can be our cabin boy. There is treasure to be found—and I mean to find it!"

"I will go with you, Trelawney," the doctor replied, "on one condition."

"And what is that?" asked the squire.

"That you tell no one—not a living soul—of our objective, or all will be lost."

"Livesey," said the squire solemnly, "I shall be as silent as the grave."

One month later, I said goodbye to Mother and the inn where I had lived all my life, and traveled by mail coach to Bristol to join Squire Trelawney and Dr. Livesey.

The squire had bought a ship called the *Hispaniola,* and had fitted it out so that it was ready to sail. By the time I arrived, a crew had been assembled. The man in charge was called Captain Smollett, and the crew had been hired with the help of an old ship's cook named Long John Silver, who now ran a tavern in Bristol.

"When do we sail?" I asked Squire Trelawney.

"Tomorrow!" the squire said with shining eyes. "For now, I need you to take this message to Silver."

He handed me a note, and showed me how to find Silver's tavern, the Spy-glass.

As I walked along the docks, I tried to take in all that was before me. Sailors—many with ponytails, rings in their ears, and curling whiskers—swaggered along the quayside. Ships of every size were docked here, some with sailors hanging off the rigging, singing loudly.

Although I had lived by the shore all my life, I felt that I had never really been near the ocean until now. I was about to sail off to an unknown island, in search of buried treasure! I could barely contain my excitement.

The Spy-glass Tavern had neat red drapes and a newly painted sign. I peered through the window and saw the customers were nearly all seafaring men. I was almost afraid to enter. But enter I did, and I asked for the landlord.

At the Sign of the Spy-glass

Long John Silver was a tall man. His left leg was cut off at the hip, and he had a crutch under his left shoulder, which he managed with great skill. He was smiling and friendly—but something about him worried me. Could Long John Silver be the one-legged man Billy Bones had been so afraid of?

I introduced myself, and handed Silver the note from Squire Trelawney. He read it and looked at me. "You're the new cabin boy!" he said. "Pleased to meet you!"

He accompanied me back to Squire Trelawney's lodgings, where the squire told him to have all hands on deck and ready to sail.

"Aye, aye, sir," Long John replied.

When Long John had gone, I boarded the ship with Squire Trelawney and Dr. Livesey. Something was troubling Captain Smollett, so he took us to his cabin to speak with the squire and Dr. Livesey in private.

"It seems," Captain Smollett began, "that we are on a treasure voyage, and I don't like it. And everyone on board, except me, has known about it from the start."

"What are you worried about?" asked the squire.

"We are in danger of mutiny," Smollett replied. "The entire crew know about the treasure map. They also know where the gunpowder and weapons are kept, so we must lock it away in a secret place."

Smollett got his way, but the squire thought he was a coward.

We set sail just after dawn the next morning. I was worn out from the excitement of the previous day, and had not had much sleep, but I would not have missed being on deck. The boatswain summoned the crew to turn the capstan bars and hoist the anchor. As they turned, the men sang a song I'd heard sung many times:

"Fifteen men on the dead man's chest,
Yo-ho-ho and a bottle of rum!"

As the voyage got underway, I began spending time with Long John Silver. He often invited me to join him in the galley, which he kept as clean as a new pin.

"Come away, Hawkins," he would say. "Come and have a yarn with John."

He told me stories of his many voyages, and told me about his parrot, Cap'n Flint, who sat in a cage in the corner of the galley.

"I named him for the famous buccaneer," Long John told me. "And he's predicting the success of our voyage, aren't you, Cap'n?"

In reply, the parrot shrieked, "Pieces of eight! Pieces of eight! Pieces of eight!" over and over again.

"That bird has been on voyages all over the world, Jim," Long John told me. "He's seen more gold coins than either of us could count. That's why he shouts about pieces of eight all the time."

Long John was so warm and friendly that I could not help but trust him and put my earlier suspicions aside.

What I Heard in the Apple Barrel

One evening, I was hungry and went to the apple barrel looking for something to eat. There were hardly any apples left, so I had to crawl right to the bottom to get one. It was dark and warm in the barrel. I had worked hard that day and was very tired. I curled up and fell asleep, rocked by the waves beneath the ship.

I was wakened by the sound of voices just above me. Long John Silver was talking with some of the crewmen.

"I was Flint's quartermaster," he said, "because of my peg leg. You know, I lost my leg in the same attack as the one where Pew was blinded. We were both Flint's men."

"Flint was the best," said another sailor. I recognized his voice—it was Dick, one of Long John's recruits, and the youngest sailor on board.

"Yes," agreed the coxswain, Israel Hands, "not like this Smollett. I've had about as much of him as I can stand. We have enough of Flint's men on board, Long John— when are we going to take over?"

My blood ran cold. Not only was Long John a pirate, but he had recruited pirates as crewmen. And they were planning a mutiny against the others. Captain Smollett had been right all along!

"We'll wait until the time is right," Long John was saying. "When we've got the treasure, we can do away with Smollett and the rest. Will you join us, Dick?"

Dick agreed to join the pirates, and Long John sent him to fetch a pitcher of rum.

Just then the lookout cried, "Land ho!" and there was a rush of running feet across the deck. In the commotion, I managed to climb out of the apple barrel unnoticed.

There was an island up ahead, and Captain Smollett asked if anyone recognized it.

Long John Silver said he did. "I was cook on a trading ship that stopped here once. Skeleton Island, it's called."

It was the island on the treasure map!

After working out where the best landing spot was, the captain dismissed Long John, telling him they might need his help later. Long John smiled at me as he went, and I hoped he could not see from my face how frightened of him I felt now.

Later, I asked to speak with the captain, Squire Trelawney, and Dr. Livesey in Captain Smollett's cabin. When I told them what I had heard while I was in the apple barrel, they were all grateful. The captain did not seem surprised, but said there was little we could do until we knew how many men were against us.

"You are an observant lad, Jim," said Dr. Livesey, "and you can be more help to us than anyone. The men trust you, so you will be able to assist us in discovering who is friend and who is foe."

I promised to do all I could.

The Man of the Island

By the following morning, we lay about half a mile off Skeleton Island. From this distance I could see that much of the island was thickly wooded, and that hills rose up behind the trees.

Led by Long John Silver, thirteen sailors volunteered to row ashore to explore the island. At the last minute, I jumped into one of the boats; I tried to curl up and hide, but Long John caught sight of me.

When I realized that I would be alone on the island with Long John and his men, terror took hold of me. The moment we landed, I leapt from the boat and ran.

I was crouching in a thicket when I heard voices. I peered out to see Long John Silver talking with Tom, one of the sailors loyal to the captain.

"It's up to you," Long John was saying. "You can throw your lot in with the captain, or you can save your neck and join us."

"I would sooner lose my own hand than betray the captain," Tom replied. He turned and walked away.

Grabbing a tree branch for balance, Long John flung his crutch at Tom's back. Tom gasped and fell to the ground. Long John, swift as a monkey even though he no longer had his crutch, was on top of Tom in seconds. He drew out his knife and plunged it into Tom's back. Then he stood up and whistled—a signal to his men.

I took a chance and stole away as quietly as I could, then ran for my life.

I ran as I had never run before, not caring where I went as long as it was away from Long John and his men. I soon realized I was lost and had no idea how to get back to the ship. Even if I had known the way, I was sure the pirates would kill me as soon as they saw me.

Suddenly I felt my heart almost leap from my body—a strange, shaggy figure was moving between the trees. Hesitantly, the figure emerged. He was unlike any man I had seen before. He fell to his knees, his hands clasped.

"Who are you?" I asked.

"I'm poor Ben Gunn, I am," he replied, "and I haven't spoken to another soul for three long years."

He told me he had been one of Captain Flint's men. His shipmates had left him marooned on the island.

"Is that Flint's ship in the harbor?" he asked.

"Flint is dead," I told him, "but some of his men are on our crew. Long John Silver is their leader."

At the mention of Long John's name, Ben began to tremble. "Did he send you looking for me?" he asked.

I assured him that he hadn't, and told him the whole story of our voyage. He asked if Squire Trelawney would give him safe passage home if he helped find the treasure.

"I'm sure he would help you," I assured Ben.

How the Ship Was Abandoned

Ben Gunn and I were making our way to the *Hispaniola* when I heard cannon fire. I ran toward the sound, and saw a red flag fluttering above the trees.

"It's the old log fort," Ben told me. "Your friends must have come ashore, and the mutineers are attacking them."

"I must join them," I told Ben.

"You know where to find me if you want me," Ben said. As a cannon ball exploded in the sand nearby, we fled in different directions.

At the fort, I was welcomed warmly by Dr. Livesey, Squire Trelawney, Captain Smollett, and the crewmen who had stayed loyal to them. Dr. Livesey told me what had happened after I left the ship.

Not all the mutineers had gone ashore with Long John Silver—six remained aboard the *Hispaniola*, led by Israel Hands. Dr. Livesey knew about the log fort from Flint's map, so while Captain Smollett and Squire Trelawney held Israel Hands and his men at bay, Dr. Livesey and the loyal crewmen rowed supplies out to the island. Eventually all our men were safe in the fort. The *Hispaniola* was now in the mutineers' hands, and they had begun firing at the fort, just as Ben Gunn had said.

I told Dr. Livesey about Ben Gunn, and he was most interested in how Gunn might help us. Captain Smollett, however, was more concerned with defending the fort.

From the *Hispaniola*, the mutineers continued bombarding the fort until sunset. When it grew dark, we could see the glow of a fire in the woods, where Long John and his men were camped. I was very tired, and slept soundly that night.

I awoke the next morning to hear the shout, "Flag of truce!" I looked out and saw Silver approaching the fort. He wanted to strike a deal with Captain Smollett.

"Give us the map," said Long John, "and we will see that you get back to England safely."

"I'll make no bargains with you," replied Smollett.

Silver's eyes bulged with fury, and he vowed to attack the fort. "Them that die'll be the lucky ones," he warned.

At midday, as the blistering sun beat down, four pirates brandishing cutlasses leapt across the fence and swarmed over the fort. Musket shots rang out from the woods. Our men, armed and ready, returned their fire.

The log fort was full of smoke, and cries of pain mingled with the boom of musket shots. I grabbed a cutlass and ran out to face the pirates. Within moments, we had beaten them back. Of the four who came over the fence, only one survived. He was now clambering back over as quickly as he could.

Two of our men were lost in the fight, and the captain was seriously injured. We waited for another attack, but none came.

The Cruise of the Coracle

That afternoon, Dr. Livesey left the fort, and took the treasure map with him. He didn't say, but I guessed that he was going out to look for Ben Gunn.

The heat inside the log house was stifling, and I was desperate to escape. I took some sea biscuits and a pair of pistols and crept out of the fort. Looking toward the shore I could see the *Hispaniola* and hear the men's voices. They were laughing and shouting at one another.

As I made my way down to the shore, I saw something else. Beside a rock, hidden under some hides, was a coracle—a small boat—which I knew belonged to Ben Gunn. A plan began to take shape in my mind. If I could cut the *Hispaniola*'s anchor ropes, the ship would be cast adrift and would then run aground. The pirates would be trapped on the island.

As darkness fell, a cold fog rolled in. It gave me enough cover to carry out my plan without fear of being seen. I launched the coracle and slowly paddled toward the ship. Luckily, the tide carried me right up beside the anchor cable. I caught hold of it and slipped out my sailor's knife. I cut the cable, strand by strand, and the ship slid out to sea.

As the ship creaked past me, I managed to grab hold of a line and pull myself up to a window. Peering inside, I saw Israel Hands locked in a vicious struggle with another sailor. I quickly dropped back into my little boat as the ship drew away from me.

Suddenly, the coracle lurched to one side, and I was caught in the powerful tide. I lay flat in the bottom of the boat and prayed that my Maker might save my life as I was carried out to the open ocean.

I must have lain there for hours, being beaten about by the waves. I was terrified, but so worn out that I could not help falling asleep. I dreamt of my home, and the Admiral Benbow Inn.

It was broad daylight when I awoke. I was near the southwest corner of the island, and still could not control the coracle. Then, as the current took me around the tip of the island, the *Hispaniola* swung into view!

Her sails were flapping gently, and she was drifting slowly toward me. As the ship drew closer, all seemed quiet—I could not see a soul on deck.

Suddenly the *Hispaniola* was above me. I heaved myself aboard just in time, as the mighty ship smashed the tiny coracle to pieces.

It was eerily quiet on board. Israel Hands and the man I had seen him fighting with hours before both lay on the bloodstained deck. Hands was still alive, but the other man was lifeless and stiff as a spike.

I hauled down the Jolly Roger and flung it overboard, then turned to Hands. He asked me for brandy and help with his wounds. I was ready to help him—if he would help me to sail the *Hispaniola* to a safe anchorage.

Israel Hands

I went below to get food and drink for Hands, and I took a silk handkerchief from my own trunk to bind up his bleeding thigh. As I was returning, I saw him crawl painfully across the deck to reach for a knife concealed in a coil of rope, then hide it in his jacket. I was glad that I still had the two pistols I had taken from the fort.

Hands helped me sail the ship to the north of the island. As I was steering toward the shore, a sudden feeling of terror seized me, and I turned around.

Hands was halfway toward me, with the knife in his right hand. I tried to fire one of my pistols, but the powder was damp, and it would not shoot.

Hands lunged at me, and I screamed and leapt aside. In desperation I scrambled up the rigging, and managed to reload my weapons. Hands climbed toward me, the dagger clenched between his teeth.

"One more step and I'll blow your brains out, Hands!" I shouted at him, holding my pistols ready.

"Jim," he replied, "I reckon we're both done for, you and I."

He flung the dagger at me, and it struck me right on the shoulder.

In the horrid pain and surprise of the moment, both my pistols went off, then fell from my hands and into the ocean below. With a choked cry, Israel Hands fell backward and plummeted headfirst into the water.

I was now alone on the *Hispaniola*. I leapt down from the rigging and then waded ashore to make my way to the log fort.

It was dark by the time I got there. As I crept inside, I heard snoring, and felt comforted to know that my friends were sleeping peacefully.

But suddenly a shrill voice shrieked, "Pieces of eight! Pieces of eight!" It was Long John Silver's parrot!

"Who goes?" called Silver.

Silver held a lamp up to my face. "Jim Hawkins!" he said. "Have you come to join us?"

I was surrounded by pirates. My friends were nowhere to be seen, and I feared the worst. But I learnt that they had surrendered the fort—and the treasure map—to the pirates. I could not believe they had given in so easily.

"You are in a bad way," I told the pirates. "I've cut the ship adrift. You have no way of leaving the island now."

The pirates were furious, and two of them came at me. Silver held them off, but from the way they spoke to him, I could tell they no longer respected him.

"They want to get rid of me," Silver admitted when we were alone. "I'm on the squire's side now, and I'll save your life if I can—if you will help me."

If the pirates discovered that Long John had switched sides, they would kill us. My only hope was to throw my lot in with him.

"I'll do what I can," I told him.

The Voice Among the Trees

Next morning, Dr. Livesey came to the log fort to treat the sick and wounded pirates.

"We have a new boarder," Silver told him, pushing me forward.

Dr. Livesey was surprised to see me. After he had dressed the pirates' wounds and given them their medicine, he asked to speak with me privately. Silver told us to talk outside, near the fence, so the others would not hear us.

"Doctor," he said, as he accompanied us outside, "Jim will tell you how I saved his life." Then, in a whisper, he added, "I'm hoping you might do the same for me."

Behind us, the pirates began shouting and calling Silver a traitor for making deals with the doctor. It looked as if he had completely lost control of the men.

We could see that Silver was shaken. Eyes downcast, he sat on a tree stump out of earshot of the doctor and I.

As soon as we were alone, I told Dr. Livesey what had happened aboard the *Hispaniola*, and where the ship was now anchored. He was surprised and relieved to know that the ship was safe.

"You've saved our lives again, Jim," he said. "You can be sure that we will not let you lose yours."

He called Silver over to join us, "Keep the boy close, and shout if you need assistance. I'm off to seek help."

He shook my hand, nodded to Silver, then turned and left.

I returned to the fort to have breakfast with Silver and the pirates. Then with picks and shovels we set out to look for the treasure. I had a rope around my waist and was led by Long John Silver. He and all the others were armed with cutlasses and guns.

The men were talking about the map. On the back was written,

"Tall tree, spyglass shoulder, bearing a
point to the north of north by northeast.
Skeleton Island east by southeast by east ten feet."

The men were excited and raced ahead. Then suddenly one of them screamed. He had found a human skeleton lying on the ground. Some shreds of sea cloth still clung to the bones. Oddly, his feet pointed in one direction, and his outstretched hands pointed exactly opposite.

"This is one of Flint's jokes," Silver said, looking at his compass. "He's pointing east southeast by east, just like the map says. This is the way to the treasure!"

At that moment, a thin, trembling voice sang out,

"Fifteen men on the dead man's chest,
Yo-ho-ho and a bottle of rum!"

The men turned pale with terror. "Flint's song!" someone whispered. Silver was so frightened, his teeth were chattering, but he declared, "I was never scared of Flint when he was alive, and by the powers, I'll face him when he's dead! Let's get that treasure!"

The Fall of the Chieftain

The men broke into a run, and Long John hobbled to keep up with them.

All at once we came to a dead halt. Before us was a deep hole, made some time ago—grass had already begun to grow along its sides. At the bottom was the broken handle of a pickax and several boards. One of them was marked with the word "Walrus"—the name of Flint's ship.

It was clear to all of us: the treasure was gone.

Long John knew the men would turn on him. He began edging us away from them, and gave me one of his pistols. "Stand by for trouble," he muttered under his breath.

Meanwhile, the men had jumped into the pit and had begun scrabbling around. One of them found a single gold coin. He held it up, swearing, and passed it to the others.

"Two guineas!" someone roared. "That's our treasure, is it? This is all your fault, Silver!" The angry pirates scrambled out of the hole and came at us, their weapons drawn.

Just then—crack! crack! crack!—three musket shots rang out from the thicket behind us. Two of the pirates fell dead; the others turned and ran.

Dr. Livesey, Ben Gunn, and a loyal sailor named Abraham Gray emerged from the thicket. They had saved our lives.

"Thank you kindly, Doctor," gasped Long John Silver. "You came just in the nick of time. And you," he went on, turning to Ben Gunn, "it was you singing in the woods! You surely got me, Ben!"

Dr. Livesey smiled kindly at Ben. "Ben here was a hero from beginning to end," he said. And he told us how Ben had managed to come upon the treasure months before we had arrived on the *Hispaniola*—it was the handle of his pickax that lay at the bottom of the pit. Bit by bit, he had taken the treasure back to his hideout. So the treasure map was useless—and Dr. Livesey knew that when he had given the map to Long John.

We then made our way to Ben's cave to see the treasure for ourselves, where Captain Smollett and Squire Trelawney were waiting for us. The cave was surprisingly large and airy, with a little freshwater spring running through, overhung with green ferns. In a far corner I could see great heaps of glistening gold coins and heavy stacks of gold bars—we had finally found our treasure.

Long John saluted Captain Smollett, and told him he was ready to return to duty aboard the *Hispaniola*.

"Ah!" said the captain, and he said nothing more.

What a supper I had that night, and how happy I was to have all my friends around me again, and know that we were all safe. Long John sat a little way to the side, but he ate heartily and even joined in our laughter from time to time. He had become the same polite, smiling man he had been at the start of our voyage.

The next morning, we began putting the treasure into sacks and loading it onto the *Hispaniola*. There were coins from every part of the world—doubloons and guineas and moidores and strange pieces from the Orient. It gave me great pleasure to sort them.

We knew that there were three pirates still on the island, but we could not risk another mutiny by taking them with us. We left them food, tools, medicine, and musket powder. Then we boarded the ship, taking Ben Gunn and Long John with us, and set sail for home.

I cannot express the joy I felt as I stood and watched Treasure Island disappear from view.

We were short of men, so we headed for the nearest port in South America to take on extra crew. When we boarded the *Hispaniola* again, Ben Gunn stood alone on deck. Silver had gone, taking with him one sack of treasure. We were pleased to be rid of him so cheaply.

We had a good voyage home, and we each had a good share of the treasure. Ben Gunn spent his in a matter of weeks, but he was given some employment and still lives in our town, singing in the church choir on Sundays and saints' days.

I heard nothing more of Long John Silver. But sometimes I dream of that wretched island and, as I sit up in my bed, I can hear the voice of Silver's parrot screeching in my ear:

"Pieces of eight! Pieces of eight!"

About the Author

Robert Louis Stevenson was born in Scotland in 1850. His family was famed for designing and building lighthouses. Robert initially studied engineering at the University of Edinburgh to follow in his family's footsteps, but then chose to devote his life to writing and traveling. On his vast travels he sailed to France, Belgium, New York City, and California. His joy of the salty sea air and thrill of adventure eventually led him on a three-year journey across the Pacific, where he visited Hawaii, Tahiti, New Zealand, and the Samoan Islands. He eventually settled on the Samoan Islands, where he spent the remainder of his life. He died in 1894 and was buried in a spot overlooking his beloved ocean.

Other titles in the Classic Collection series:

ALICE'S ADVENTURES IN WONDERLAND   LITTLE WOMEN   THE THREE MUSKETEERS

Editor: Lauren Taylor
Designer: Izzy Langridge
Cover typography: Matthew Kelly

Copyright © QEB Publishing, Inc. 2011

First published in the United States in 2011 by
QEB Publishing, Inc.
3 Wrigley, Suite A
Irvine, CA 92618

www.qed-publishing.co.uk

Library of Congress Cataloging-in-Publication Data

Randall, Ronne.
  Treasure Island / by Robert Louis Stevenson ; retold by Ronne Randall.
      p. cm. -- (Classics collection)
  Summary: A shortened, simplified version of the story in which an innkeeper's son finds a treasure map that leads him to a pirate's fortune.
  ISBN 978-1-60992-036-4 (library bound)
  [1. Buried treasure--Fiction. 2. Pirates--Fiction. 3. Adventure and adventurers--Fiction.] I. Stevenson, Robert Louis, 1850-1894. Treasure Island. II. Title.
  PZ7.R1584Tr 2012
  [E]--dc22

                                        2010053355

ISBN 978 1 60992 298 6 (hardback)

Printed in China